....Thy Kingdom Come, Thy Will Be Done

Kingdom of the Blessed

EVANGELIST COLLETTE
CHINYERE NLEMCHI

Copyright © 2024 by Evangelist Collette Chinyere Nlemchi

ISBN: 978-1-77883-394-6 (Paperback)

All rights reserved. No part of this publication may be reproduced, distributed, or transmitted in any form or by any means, including photocopying, recording, or other electronic or mechanical methods, without the prior written permission of the publisher, except in the case brief quotations embodied in critical reviews and other noncommercial uses permitted by copyright law.

The views expressed in this book are solely those of the author and do not necessarily reflect the views of the publisher, and the publisher hereby disclaims any responsibility for them.

BookSide Press
877-741-8091
www.booksidepress.com
orders@booksidepress.com

Table of Contents

Chapter 1	Thy Will Is The Best	3
Chapter 2	Prayer To My Heavenly Father	4
Chapter 3	Praying For My Children	5
Chapter 4	Obedient And Humble	6
Chapter 5	Gratitude	7
Chapter 6	What Is Jesus To Me.?	8
Chapter 7	I Am Victorious	9
Chapter 8	My Impossibilities Are Now Possible	
Chapter 9	The Prince Of Heaven	11
Chapter 10	Servants Of The Most High God.	12
Chapter 11	Mystical Wonders	13
Chapter 12	Thou Maket A Way	14
Chapter 13	Darkness Is Defeated	15
Chapter 14	Praise Is My Name	16
Chapter 15	Protection Prayers	17
Chapter 16	Increase My Greatness	18
Chapter 17	Thy Wisdom Is Infinite	19
Chapter 18	Thou Oh! Lord Is Irreplaceable	20
Chapter 19	Be Patient Says The Lord	21
Chapter 20	Thy Holy Presence	22
Chapter 21	God Of Miracles	23
Chapter 22	Wonderfully Made	24
Chapter 23	Healing My Body System	25
Chapter 24	Satanic Powers Arrested	26
Chapter 25	Psalm 23. The Lord Is My Shepherd	27
Chapter 26	Everlasting Kingdom	28
Chapter 27	Go Thou Before Me	29
Chapter 28	The Light That Shines	30
Chapter 29	Oh! My Ancestors	31
Chapter 30	Everlasting Praises.	32

1. *Thy Will Is The Best*

The will of God will never take you,
Where the grace of God cannot keep you,
Where the arms of God cannot support you,
Where the riches of God cannot supply your needs,
Where the power of God cannot endow you.

The will of God will never take you,
Where the Spirit of God cannot work through you,
Where the wisdom of God cannot teach you,
Where the army of God cannot protect you,
Where the hands of God cannot mold you.

The will of God will never take you,
Where the love of God cannot enfold you,
Where the mercies of God cannot sustain you,
Where the peace of God cannot calm your fears,
Where the authority of God cannot overrule for you.

The will of God will never take you,
Where the comfort of God cannot dry your tears,
Where the Word of God cannot feed you,
Where the miracles of God cannot be done for you,
Where the omnipresence of God cannot find you.

Author Unknown

2. *Prayer To My Heavenly Father*

Oh! Heavenly Father, the Creator of the Universe.
I bow down for you and I Glorify thy Holy Name.
I thank you for all you have done for me and Family.
Be it small or Big, I thank you.
I also thank you for many more blessings coming on my way.

You are the greatest that has ever lived.
Thou, Oh! Lord will forgive all my sins.
Protection from Dangerous and irresponsible Creatures.
Your Visible and Invisible Angels are at work.
And I shall accomplish all my dreams.

There is no Power Bigger than you.
I Honor and glorify thy Holy Name.
Because you are powerful and Glorious.
Oh! Master Designer, Organize my life.
Thou, shall go before me and make crooked places straight.

Thou Oh! Lord shall send prosperity Angels on my pathway.
All Sicknesses and Diseases in my body, you are arrested IJN.
I have no choice but to serve the Lord My God.
All my Needs both Known and Unknown are Supplied IJN.
Lead thou me to the right direction and deliver me from all evil Amen.

EVANGELIST COLLETTE NLEMCHI.

3. PRAYING FOR MY CHILDREN

Praying for your Children is very important and it brings great results. As you follow this prayer model, call your Children by the name as you pray for them. (Isa 54:13). All my children shall be taught by the LORD, and great shall be the peace of my Children. In Righteousness they shall be established and they shall be far from oppression; for they shall not fear; from terror. (Jer 31:16-17). Because, I delight in thy commandments, You said my Children will enjoy your blessings day by day.

Psalm 112: 1-2). You promised you will pour out Your Spirit upon my seed, Your blessings upon my offspring and that someday they will say, "I am the Lord's."

(Is 44:3-5). You said that You will never forget them, because their names are engraved on the palms of your hands and you will destroy anything that tries to destroy them.

(Isa 39: 16-17) Father, You promised to save my children, and I claim it.

Agent of Satan that are trying to block the glorious beginning of my Children this year, I command you to somersault, run mad and die in Jesus name.

Oh! Holy Spirit, move into the lives of my Children this year and let them experience spiritual revival in things of God, in Jesus Name.

There should be a Remarkable achievement at the homes of my Children In Jesus Name.

My Children shall not fall into wrong hands In Jesus Name. My Children shall be attracted to Spiritual and good people In Jesus Name.

Their Relationships, Education, Behavior and Spirituality shall receive Revival In Jesus Name.

EVANGELIST COLLETTE NLEMCHI.

4. *OBEDIENT AND HUMBLE*

Oh! PRINCE of Heaven who Created the World, I am Obedient to You.
On my Knees I bow down to the King of Kings.
And I say, Hallo be thy Holy Name.
Thy will shall be done on Earth whether Satan like it or not.
I bow down for you, mighty and Holy One.

Thou Oh! Lord shall make a way in this life of Confusion.
It is only you who knows all the Mysteries and the Right Direction.
Only you has the Power to solve these puzzles.
And I say once again, let your will be done.
Give me Courage to take whatever the outcome based on your Will.
Thou shall speedily provide the Answer.

What is your will I ask? And what is your Decision?
Your Decision, in this world of Confusion.
Where are your Angels? You promised to send them to me.
Speedily dispatch your Angels to solve my problems.
Thou shall destroy any curses upon me and send back to Cursers.
Blessings upon Blessings I shall possess.
In the mighty name of Jesus, I pray, Amen.

EVANGELIST COLLETTE NLEMCHI.

5. GRATITUDE

Oh! Prince of Heaven, I thank you for all you have done for me.
I am grateful for the blessings in my life.
I thank you for the life I live.
I thank you for my Children and their Transformation.
I thank you for the Angels that are constantly guiding me.

Thou has fought numerous battle for me against my Attackers.
I thank you for guiding my Footsteps.
I thank you for Protection.
Lord, I thank you for your Holliness.
Lord I thank you for all my blessings known and Unknown.

I thank you for thy ways. Thy ways are Different.
The way you do things are beyond human Understanding.
I thank you for giving me and my Children Longer and Glorious Days.
I thank you for Reversing Curses in my Life.
I thank you for giving me good health for me and my Children.

I thank you for Everything you have done
and more on the Way.
You heal my Sicknesses and Diseases, Lord, I thank you.
You gave me Supernatural Faith, Lord I Thank You.

EVANGELIST COLLETTE NLEMCHI.

6. WHAT IS JESUS TO ME.?

Jesus is everything to me.
Jesus is the Song I Sing.
Jesus is the King of Glory.
Jesus is the Unfathomable Sea.
Jesus is my Director.
Jesus is the Protector of my Life.
Jesus is my Encourager and Comforter.
Jesus is my Judge and Lawyer who pleads my Case.
Jesus is my Repair Person, who fixes all my broken stuff.
Jesus is my Protector.
Jesus is the Author and Finisher of my Faith.
Jesus is my Power when I am Weak.
Jesus is the Lord of my Life.
Jesus is my Provider.
Jesus is my Everlasting Father.
Jesus Answer all my Prayers.
Jesus is the Light when I face darkness.
Jesus is my Supplier.
Jesus, Jesus, Jesus.
Jesus I love You Forever.

EVANGELIST COLLETTE NLEMCHI.

7. I AM VICTORIOUS

I am Victorious because I put my trust in God.
I distance myself from workers of Iniquities and the Wicked.
Today, the Lord has blessed me with Incredible Strength.
I will march forward with the Brave.
Also in your Power, I am a Champion among the Champions.

Heavenly Father you have plans for me.
You have a plan of Blessing me and my Seeds and I Claim it IJN.
You have a plan of Increase for me and I Claim it In Jesus Name.
You have a plan of Enlarging my Coast and I claim it In Jesus Name.
And I ask? Can your Plans for me be Removed or Overthrown? The Answer is NO. Thy plans for me Oh! Heaven, cannot be Removed.

I cried out to the Lord my God and he answered me.
He will straighten my Spirit and I shall stand firm.
I release the guilt of Unforgiven Sins.
My Winds shall be cleaned from undeserved Conflicts.
I let go of Grudges and Resentments and I Forgive.

EVANGELIST COLLETTE NLEMCHI.

8. MY IMPOSSIBILITIES ARE NOW POSSIBLE

You are the Pillar that holdeth my life.
Thou are Powerful and thou are Wonderful.
You made my Impossibilities become possible.
Thou Oh! Lord is Powerful.
When Storms of life comes, Lord You Rescued Me.

Honor and Favor will envelope my life, You are Powerful.
You Transformed my Life, You are Miraculous.
You answered my Prayers, you are Powerful.
I will not dwell in the past because my future is in your Hands.
I know my chosen purpose will be fulfilled.

Thou, Oh! Lord is the source of all Wisdom.
Greatness and Love shall follow me.
I shall honor your Majestic and Supernatural Existence.
Great is your faithfulness as I embark in this Journey of faith.
I therefore lay all my burdens, worries and Fear at the throne of, perfection and the case is closed In Jesus Name.

EVANGELIST COLLETTE NLEMCHI.

9. <u>THE PRINCE OF HEAVEN</u>

Oh! Prince of Heaven, you are Honorable.
Thou, holdest the whole world at your hands.
You are so Powerful.
And you are so Wonderful.
What you cannot do does not Exist.
Power of all Powers. Praise be to your Holy Name.

When I think about your mysteries, it makes me to wonder.
Power of all Powers, you are wonderful.
Thank you for all your blessings. Big or Small I thank you.
Thou Oh! Lord is my strength when I am weak.
I come to you with a heart full of gratitude.
Shield me from any kind of Evil and guide my steps.

I surrender all my plans and desires to you.
I seek you Oh! Lord as a precious Jewel.
You are the Treasure that I seek.
You pick me up when I fall down.
Worthy is your name, Oh! Jesus the Lamb of God.

EVANGELIST COLLETTE NLEMCHI

10. <u>SERVANTS OF THE MOST HIGH GOD.</u>

Oh! Heavenly Father, I am your Servant and I will do your work.
Though I have come a long way, I will carry the Cross of Life.
I am a Servant and I will do your work and answer the Call.
I will bring good news without any grudge.
I am a child of the most high God.

Oh! Lord, your power is unlimited and your strength has no boundaries. I thank you for all you have done in my Life.
Your Supreme Power of Miracles Baffles me.
God of Impossibilities. Make my impossible situations possible.
Thou Oh! Lord, have silenced the tongues of the Enemies.
I have heard and I have Answered. Expect Miracles. God Loves You.

I am a Chosen Vessel and God's plans in my life must be fulfilled. You my Enemies, you will fall inside the Satanic Grave you have dug for me and my family In Jesus Name.
God of Powers, Empower me to do the Extraordinary Things In Jesus Name.
Thy Name shall be glorified, whether Satan Like it or Not.

EVANGELIST COLLETTE NLEMCHI.

11. *MYSTICAL WONDERS*

Mighty One, you are more than what people say you are.
Your Creation makes me to Wonder.
The Oceans and the Rivers are Singing Alleluia.
The Trees and the Flowers are Clapping their hands.
They are all praising your Holliness.
Wonderful, it is only you who understand their Languages.

You have the whole World in your hands. You are more than Powerful.
You made the Sun, the Moon and the Stars. You are Wonderful.
You are the Commander of the Universe, you are Glorious.
You made The Heavens and the Earth, You are Miraculous.
Holy is your Name, Oh! Power of all Powers.

Thou Oh! Lord, has made a way, where there is no way.
And I know Heaven is my Destination.
Thou shall not forsake those, who diligently serve thee.
Thou shall organize my life and make my ways straight.
Omnipotent God, You are More Than What People say you are.

EVANGELIST COLLETTE NLEMCHI.

12. *THOU MAKET A WAY*

Omnipotent Father, thou will make a Way.
Father of all Fathers, thou will make a way.
Ancient of Days, thou will make a way.
God of All Powers, thou will make a way.
I am that I am, thou will make a way.
Impossibility Diffuser, thou will make a way.
Holy of all Hollies, Thou will make a way.
Miraculous Father, thou will make a way.
Thou goet before me and maket Crooked places Straight,
Holy Master, thou will make a way.
The God of Powers, thou will make a way.
The Author of Redemption, thou will make a way.
The Speaker of Revelation, thou will make a way.
The Greatest Ever Lived, thou will make a way.
The Mysterious Deity, thou will make a way.
Universal Commander, thou will make a way.
My Known and Unknown needs, thou will make a way.
I claim all my Needs In Jesus Name.

                EVANGELIST COLLETTE NLEMCHI.

13. *DARKNESS IS DEFEATED*

Oh! Ye Darkness, thou art defeated at the throne of Perfection.
All Evil is destroyed In Jesus Name.
Goodness and Mercy shall follow me In Jesus Name.
I shall dwell in the House of the Lord Forever and Ever Amen.
The word of God gives me strength to conquer any situation.
I am vigilant, therefore, no Enemy will harm me In Jesus Name.

The word of God is a shield for me and my Family in Jesus Name.
My Home shall be free from Evil, Misery, Scarcity and Illness IJN.
By Relying on the word of God, all evil should flee In Jesus Name.
With the Word of God on my lips, am vigilant and no Enemy will harm me In Jesus Name.

Father of all Fathers, thy Kingdome come and let thy will be done.
My name is Praise and my full time Job is Praise.
I will praise your Holy Name all the days of my Life.
I have no choice, I will continue to praise and exalt thy holy Name.
I see what many did not see.
Everlasting Praise is in my lips, Oh! Holy One.

EVANGELIST COLLETTE NLEMCHI.

14. *PRAISE IS MY NAME*

Holy Master, I will Praise and glorify you in this life I live.
You are the Greatest that has ever lived or existed,
There is none like you. Ancient of Days, thy will be done.
Creator of this World, I praise your Holy Name.
Mankind Come and Go but Oh! Heaven thou livet Forever.
Endless is your Name. No beginning and No End.

The Holly Angels are Singing Praises 24 hrs.
Oh! Heaven, you are more than what people say you are.
You cannot be described , challenged or Overtaken.
The Power of all Powers, I call thee, Everlasting Deity, I Salute.
Mountain Mover, thou shall move my Mountains.

Holly of Hollies, Thank you for Answered Prayers.
Thou Oh! Lord shall direct my Path.
All my Problems, known and Unknown, you find me Solution.
Thou Oh! Lord shall speed up my Blessings.
When I am battling with Uncertainties, you are my Consolation.

EVANGELIST COLLETTE NLEMCHI

15. PROTECTION PRAYERS

Evil shall slay the wicked and those that hate the Righteous shall be desolate. (Perish)

The Lord Redeemet the soul of his Servants and none of them that trust in him shall Perish.

The Lord heard my cry and he brought me out from a horrible place and set my feet upon a Rock, and established my goings.

According to Matthew 5: 14-16. Jesus Christ teaches us to be the light of the world. Illuminating the darkness and bringing hope to those around us. That being said, our Christian identity is not only by attending church and reciting prayers, rather, the Church should glorify God Individually and Collectively.

Isaiah 42:8. "I am the LORD, that is my name, and my glory, I give to no other nor praise to Carved Idols."

Ps 66:2: Sing the Glory of his praise and make his praise Glorious.

Isaiah 43: There is no other Savior beside Jehovah

Proverb 53: 6. In all your ways submit to him and he will make your ways straight.

EVANGELIST COLLETTE NLEMCHI.

16. _INCREASE MY GREATNESS_

Thou Oh! Lord shall increase my Greatness, comfort me on every side.
Oh! Lord, bless me and Enlarge my Coast.
Oh! heaven, give me greater Height. In Jesus Name.
Let me know Oh! Lord, what is out there to Explore.
Let your hand be with me.
I know thy hand carry Power and Greatness.
When thy hand Carry me, my Lord, I will run and Explore like Elijah.
When the Hand of God is upon me, there will be Speed.
When you are Ridiculed and are object of people discussion, the Hand of God will lift me up.
The Mighty Hand of God is Great and I will be Mysteriously lifted by the Powerful Hand of God.
This God you see is not only a blesser, he is also a Lifter.
Everything that was lost shall return unto me. everything that was stollen shall be returned unto me.

EVANGELIST COLLETTE NLEMCHI.

17. _THY WISDOM IS INFINITE_

Oh! Lord, whose Wisdom is Infinite answer me.
Answer me as I call upon your name.
Your Wonders cannot be explained.
Thy ways are different and cannot be determined.
You are all Powerful and Wonderful.
You uplifted those that are lame.

It is all about you my Glorious Paradise.
There is no human Logic that can erase thy existence.
Because you are with me, I will Arise.
The Children are praising you, even at their recess
This is because you are the Holy of Hollies.

The believers will serve you forever.
And those who love the Lord are satisfied.
Power of all Powers, I repeat you are Powerful.
Those who love and serve thee are Justified.
Thou are Powerful and thou are Wonderful.
Hosanna to the Highest Heaven.

EVANGELIST COLLETTE NLEMCHI.

18. THOU OH! LORD IS IRREPLACEABLE

Oh! Heaven none is like you and non can Replace You.
Though they try to pull punches, Master, you are Irreplaceble.
Oh! Lord none on the surface of the earth can Replace you.
While Magicians are performing Magic, Lord you are Irresistible.
Thou Oh! Lord pick me up when I am down.

I give you thanks and praises for all my blessings.
Thou Oh! Lord destroy the Evil plans of my Enemies.
Oh! Ye my Attackers, thou are destroyed by the Angels of Light.
Holy Master Jesus, The Lamb of God, You are worthy.
Everlasting Praises I give You my Lord, Oh! King of Kings.

Thou Oh! Lord is the Treasure I seek.
Thou shall supply all my needs according to your Glory.
Master of the Universe, I salute you my Lord.
Thou has given me strength when I am weak.
With you by my side, I will not be lonely.

EVANGELIST COLLETTE NLEMCHI

19. BE PATIENT SAYS THE LORD

Oh! Ye Righteous Ones, thou shall be Patient with your Creator.
Heaven, look around to see what is best for you.
He will never abandon you with your request and wants.
He is a rewarder of those who diligently seek him.
You are everything I need.
My cup overflows with your power.
You are the Fountain and the stream of life.

Thou shall focus on the marvelous things the Lord has done for you.
Do not be Envious, thou shall count your own blessings.
He will make the World a better place for you if you seek him.
The pain and sorrows of my life is being washed away.
I will shout the shout of Faith because the Righteous live by Faith.
Even if the Wicked points fingers at me, curses me, rejects me, I am living at the Kingdom of the Blessed. And the Wicked is doomed.

I adore the Cherubis who are doing Everlasting Praises to the King.
Holy, Holy, Holy, they praise his Holy Name.
Adorations and Praises, they give him 24hrs and None Stop.
This is their full-time Job. Praises and Adorations.
Thank you Cherubis, for your Obedience to the Endless.

EVANGELIST COLLETTE NLEMCHI.

20. *THY HOLY PRESENCE*

Mighty one, thy Holy Presence Surrounds me in all I do and Say.
Organize my life and thou shall guide my Foot Steps.
Unto your Kingdom, I shall dwell.
And I will carry the Cross of Life.
Thou Oh! Lord has called us to thy Holy Temple.
This is not Brick and Mortar Temple.
This is a Spiritual Realm where the Hollies Dwellet.

As we begin to worship, we shall cleanse our hearts.
At his presence, there shall be holiness and Perfection.
As we bow down and give him Adoration.
Oh! King of Kings, I have come to thy Throne.
Receive me, and wash away all my Sins.

Everlasting Praise I give you all the days of my Life.
Thou Oh! Lord is the Speaker of Revelation.
You are also the Author of Redemption.
Oh! Glorious Paradise I salute you my Lord.
Thou are Worthy to be praised.

EVANGELIST COLLETTE NLEMCHI.

21. GOD OF MIRACLES

Thou Oh! Lord shall answer when I callet thee.
You are the Omnipotent Daddy.
What you cannot do, does not exist.
You are the Holly of Hollies.
You have answered my prayers as I callet thee.
Thank you for Answered Prayers.

Thou Oh! Lord shall give me Right Connection.
And thou Oh! Lord has given me Miracle Breakthrough.
I shall have fulfilling Transition.
Divine appointment shall be my portion.
The ways of the Lord may look Rough, but that is the right way.
There should be no mistake to abide by thy will.

Brethren, keep your Trust to the Creator of the Universe.
Thou who does the impossible, I am a member of your Kingdom.
As a Member, I shall possess my Possessions.
My Destiny must be fulfilled.
All Sicknesses and diseases, you are under Arrest.

EVANGELIST COLLETTE NLEMCHI.

22. WONDERFULLY MADE

The Creator, knows why he Created me the way I am.
That being said, I am wonderfully made for a purpose.
That purpose for my being cannot be stopped by Satanic Agents.
Though Oh! Lord shall silence the mouth of the Demon Spirits
And thou Oh! Lord shall put them where they belong.

Mess not with my anointed ones, thou have said.
And if anyone does that, they shall be doomed.
They shall be very far away from the Kingdom of the Blessed.
Oh! Kingdom of the Blessed, I am dwelling in your Mist.
Thank You Oh! King of Kings for Acceptance.

Eyes have not seen nor ear heard, what God will do for those who put their Trust in him.
The Creator shall put you at the Top and thou shall never go down.
Ye, Satanic Forces, thou has no Power over my Life and thou shall not cast me down.
I am a Child of the Creator and am Wonderfully Made.
That being said, Satanic Forces are destroyed In Jesus Name.

EVANGELIST COLLETTE NLEMCHI.

23. HEALING MY BODY SYSTEM

I come against, I stop, I reverse and I neutralize every evil presence in my bodily system.

Reproductive system, I command you to receive Healing In Jesus Name.

Nervous System, I command you to receive healing in Jesus Name.

Circulatory System, I command you to receive healing In Jesus Name.

Digestive System. I command you to receive healing In Jesus Name.

Skeletal System. I command you to receive healing. In Jesus Name.

Endocrine System. I command you to receive healing In Jesus Name.

Respiratory System. I command Healing In Jesus Name.

Muscular System. I command you to be healed In Jesus Name.

Excretory System.. I command you to be healed In Jesus Name.

Hearth/Chest… I command you to be healed In Jesus Name.

All Negative Materials circulating in my blood stream, I command you to be Evacuated In Jesus Name.

EVANGELIST COLLETTE NLEMCHI.

24. *SATANIC POWERS ARRESTED*

1. Every Evil Finger, pointing at me, I command you to wither, In Jesus name.
2. Satanic Powers wanting shame and embarrassment for me, I command you to be destroyed In Jesus Name.
3. Evil Powers, challenging the Powers of God in me, be destroyed IJN.
4. All Satanic Powers rendered against my life, I command you to be destroyed In Jesus Name.
5. Oh! Lord, destroy and disgrace the tongue of the Enemy In Jesus Name.
6. As they like cursing, let curses come upon them In Jesus Name.
7. my eyes shall see my desire upon my Enemies and my Ears shall hear my desire upon the Wicked In Jesus Name.
8. Stars of Heaven, Fight my Battles for me.
9. Oh! Angels of Paradise, Continue to Guide me In Jesus Name.

EVANGELIST COLLETTE NLEMCHI.

25. PSALM 23. THE LORD IS MY SHEPHERD

The Lord is my Shepherd, I shall not want.
He makes me to lie down, in green pastures.
He leads me beside still Waters.
And he restoreth my Soul.
He leadest me in paths of Righteousness for his name sake.
Yea, though I walk through the valley of shadow of death, I fear no evil. For thou art with me, thy rod and thy staff, they comfort me.
Thou, preparest a table before me in the presence of my Enemies.
Thou, anointed my hair with oil, my cup runneth over.
Surely goodness and mercy shall follow me all the days of my life: and I will dwell in the house of the Lord for ever.

PSALMS OF DAVID.

EVANGELIST COLLETTE NLEMCHI.

26. *EVERLASTING KINGDOM*

Thou, Oh! Lord, has an Everlasting Kingdom.
Thy Dominion endureth throughout all generations.
Mankind comet and Mankind Goet.
Thou Oh! Lord is Everlasting and thou livet forever.
The whole World is Praising Your Name.
Thou, are Powerful and thou Oh! Lord is Wonderful.

Great is thy Faithfulness, my Lord.
I know my chosen Purpose will be fulfilled.
And Miracles from the Lord will unfold in my life.
My Family will be blessed in your name.
I am planted in the house of the Lord. Ps. 92:13.
And he givet me grace to flourish like a palm tree,
And I will grow like a Ceder of Lebanon.

Blessed are the Saints that Genuinely serve and worship you.
They shall reap the reward of their labor.
Thou Oh! Lord is the lover of those who serve and worship thee.
And the Kingdom of God belongs to them.
Child of God, I will silence the tongues of the Enemies.
And I will destroy their evil plans.
Their evil will Boomerang upon their Heads.

EVANGELIST COLLETTE NLEMCHI.

27. GO THOU BEFORE ME

Their wishes and Curses, will summersault and go back to them.
OH! Heaven, thou shall go before me and Neutralize Crooked Places and Crooked People.
Upon this Rock, he said to Peter, I will build my Church and no gates of hail shall prevail.
And he said, "Mess not with my Anointed ones and to my Real Prophets do no harm."
That been said, if you mess with God's anointed, it is a dangerous Game.
The God of Heaven will fight you until he finish You.
Angels of Paradise are on guide 24hrs, protecting the Chosen Ones.
They are armed with the most dangerous and Mysterious Weapons.
To the Chosen ones, they protect and they defend.
Power of all Powers, none like you and thou shall be praised and honored.

EVANGELIST COLLETTE NLEMCHI.

28. _THE LIGHT THAT SHINES_

At the End of the Tunnel you make a Right
As you make a right, here comes the Light.
And God is the Light that Shines.
The Brightness of the Light baffles me.
I have no choice but to give thanks.

Thank you for your Glory, Wonder and Majesty.
I am the Righteousness of God in Christ Jesus.
I am full of love, and the love of God is shed in my life by the Holy Spirit.
I am a Child of God, born genuinely not of flesh and blood but of imperishable spirit.
Glory be to God to the Highest Heaven.

They will fight you, but they will fail.
I am with you and I will take care of you.
I, the Lord have spoken. (Jeremiah 1:19).
You are Holy and Anointed, and any Evil messing with the Lord's anointed is banned from Eternal Life and the case is closed.
Mess not with my anointed ones. (Psalm 105:15)

    EVANGELIST COLLETTE NLEMCHI.

29. <u>OH! MY ANCESTORS</u>

Wonderful World, Mysterious World, and Extraordinary Creatures.
Oh! Ye my Ancestors, you left behind the footprints of greatness.
Where thou Goet, no one knowet.
We have a God that Controls the Universe.
And the Mysteries around us maket me to Wonder.

When I think about my Ancestors, I ask, did you have a good journey.
Did you see the Creator of the Universe?
Did you see the Beautiful Flowers in Heaven?
How about the Numerous Angels Singing Alleluia?

Citizens of Heaven, Welcomes the Righteous.
At the Throne of Perfection they dwelet.
I am Righteous and I am Chosen.
That been said, I dwell with the Angels at the Throne of Perfection.
Thank you Lord for your Acceptance.

EVANGELIST COLLETTE NLEMCHI.

30. *EVERLASTING PRAISES.*

Let us praise the Lord, for he is worthy to be praised.
24hrs I praise my Heavenly Father with the Angels of Paradise.
Holy is your name and thou shall be praised at all times.
For good and for bad, I will praise thee.

I will enter his gates with thanksgiving, and into his courts with praise.
Be thankful unto him. And bless his name. The Lord is good and his mercy endureth forever. Psalm 100: 4,5.

"Sing praises to the Lord, who dwells in Zion! Declare His deeds among the people." Psalm 9:11.

"And my tongue shall speak of Your righteousness and of Your praise all the day long." Psalm 35:28.

"O Lord, open my lips, and my mouth shall show forth your praise." Psalm 51 15.

"Let the peoples praise You, O God, let all the people praise you." Ps.67:3.

"I will sing to the Lord as long as I live; I will sing praise to my God while I have my being." Psalm 104:33.

"I will extol You, my God, O King; and I will bless Your name forever and ever." Psalm 145:1.

EVANGELIST COLLETTE NLEMCHI.

www.ingramcontent.com/pod-product-compliance
Lightning Source LLC
LaVergne TN
LVHW041553060526
838200LV00037B/1272